The Everyday Philanthropist

Other Books by Dan Pallotta

*When Your Moment Comes: A Guide to Fulfilling Your
Dreams, by a Man Who Has Led Thousands to Greatness,*
Jodere Group, 2001

*Uncharitable: How Restraints on Nonprofits Undermine
Their Potential,* Tufts University Press, 2008

*Uncharitable: How Restraints on Nonprofits Undermine
Their Potential,* Brandeis University Press, 2022 (reissue)

*Charity Case: How the Nonprofit Community Can Stand Up
for Itself and Really Change the World,* Jossey-Bass, 2012

Sky Problems: A Frequent Flyer's Encounter with the Astral Plane,
CThings, 2019

The Everyday Philanthropist

A Better Way to Make a Better World

DAN PALLOTTA

WILEY

For general information on our other products and services or for technical support, please contact our Customer Care Department within the United States at (800) 762-2974, outside the United States at (317) 572-3993 or fax (317) 572-4002.

Wiley also publishes its books in a variety of electronic formats. Some content that appears in print may not be available in electronic formats. For more information about Wiley products, visit our web site at www.wiley.com.

Library of Congress Cataloging-in-Publication Data is Available:
ISBN 9781394190508 (Paperback)
ISBN 9781394190522 (ePub)
ISBN 9781394190515 (ePDF)

Cover Art and Design: Dan Pallotta
Cover Photo Concept: Dan Pallotta and Paiwei Wei
Cover Photo: Thomas Grassi

Interior design: Paiwei Wei
SKY10044886_032423

**To everyday philanthropists of every kind,
everywhere, who want to make a better world.**

Contents

Part Three

Part Four

Part Five

Introduction

What if everything we've been taught about charitable giving is wrong? And how much more could we do if we got it right? Those are the questions we'll address in this little but powerful guide.

The way we've been taught to think about charity and giving is remarkably counterproductive. The philosophical restrictions we place on the charities we love actually undermine them. The way we've been taught to think about our roles as charitable givers and active citizens is also remarkably misguided.

The purpose of this guide is to help you, no matter how high or low your income bracket, to see the potential of your role in civil society in a bright new light. It's to help you see how you could be a force for change in a more powerful way than you may ever have been led to believe, and, even more important, to help you see how you could be a force for changing the very way we think about change.

The economics of charitable giving can be God-awful confusing and dull. The dynamics that turn (or sometimes don't turn) the donations of millions of people into real change for millions of others can be intimidating. So, this is a clear and simple guide for people who don't have the time to think about all this, written by an expert who does. It's purposely concise and to the point. Its explanations are plainspoken. They'll demystify the mechanics of change for you. This enlightenment will leave you with a new desire to actively participate in changing the world around you—and with the confidence that you truly can.

A Sobering Opening Thought:

Ever wonder why charities aren't changing the world the way we had hoped? It's because that's not what we asked them to do. We asked them to keep their overhead and salaries low.

So guess what they did?

Part One

The
Good Citizen

Philanthropy
and You

Why Charity?

When we think about change, we think about politics, especially now. When people like former President Obama talk about creating the next generation of change-makers, they often point to politics, and create new grassroots training programs to help train and interest young people in running for elected office.

When we think of our civic duty, we think about voting or getting involved in a political campaign. We think of politics as the vehicle for change, and charity as a vehicle for being kind and generous.

This is a mistake.

Charity and the nonprofit sector are powerful vehicles for creating big change too, and sometimes even more quickly than politics can create change. And they are vehicles the average citizen can use. They are critical options for civic engagement and for any citizen interested in making a better world.

There are many examples of this:

- No Kid Hungry is actively ending child hunger in America by revolutionizing school breakfast and lunch programs.

- FoodCorps is transforming the nutritional value of those programs.

- Sightsavers is ending trachoma—one of the world's most ancient and painful diseases.

- Last Mile Health is revolutionizing basic medical services for the poor in the developing world.

- The Environmental Defense Fund is launching a satellite that can detect methane leaks at very high resolution. Methane's greenhouse gas effect

School
Breakfast Programs

A Satellites
that Detects
Methane

is 84 times more potent than carbon's. This satellite will help reduce global methane emissions 45% by 2025, delivering the same 20-year climate benefit as closing a third of the world's coal-fired power plants.

• One Acre Fund provides products and services to farmers in developing countries that substantially increase their profits and boost them out of poverty.

These changes are real. They're happening now. There are many other examples. And they're happening because average citizens are providing financial support to this work.

In fact, the average citizen would be hard-pressed to find an opportunity in politics to make more of a difference than they could by supporting some of the world's most innovative and entrepreneurial charities.

If you're interested in a holistic definition of what it means to be a good citizen, and in how to create powerful change as an individual, understanding how to give to and evaluate a charitable organization correctly is critical.

Why Giving?

Volunteering your time is satisfying and helpful and you should do it. It's good for the soul. And face-to-face interaction with charities and those they serve is incredibly fulfilling on both sides of the human equation. Donating clothing and furniture that you no longer use is wonderful.

But we're not going to change the world with volunteers and donated coats and couches. This is not how Apple, Facebook, and Tesla are changing things. What charities like the ones I mentioned previously really need is your financial support. They need many more people giving so they can expand the delivery of their powerful services to the millions of people waiting for them. They need a much stronger civil society from which to draw the financial fuel on which their growth depends, the same way Apple needs a thriving economy and a citizenry indoctrinated in the functions and benefits of their products to keep growing by leaps and bounds.

We can't get to a better world without a much stronger civil society and a much more engaged citizenry. But—and you don't need a PhD in economics to see this—getting more citizens involved and more citizens giving requires serious investment. But we don't normally think of those expenditures as "the cause"—not directly at least. And so we've been taught not to give to those things. And we've been taught that the charities that do spend money on those things are wasteful or mismanaged—that they don't really care about their constituents or cause. We actually penalize and stigmatize the organizations that try to do it correctly.

$480 Billion

Amount given in America to nonprofits annually

Americans give about $480 billion to nonprofits annually—more than any nation on earth. But only a small portion of that will go to the types of community organizations we think of as charities. The rest will go to colleges, hospitals, and religious institutions. Generous as it is, current giving isn't nearly enough to level the massively inequitable playing field between the haves and the have nots in our country and our world. This is why giving, specifically, is so important for creating real

To put it in perspective,
the money given in America to
all human services charities
in an entire year is about
equivalent to Apples' sales
in just two months.

change, and why giving intelligently—to the right organizations making the greatest difference—is critical. It's also why increasing giving is a cause that the smart philanthropist should get behind in a big way.

You Are a Philanthropist

"Me!"
Try it on.

"**P**hilanthropy" comes from the Greek *philos* and *anthropos*, for "love" of "humanity." Too often we think philanthropy is the exclusive domain of the ultra-wealthy or the big, institutional foundations created by the very rich, like the Gates or Ford Foundations. But you don't have to be a billionaire or a millionaire to be a philanthropist. When you demonstrate your love for others by making an investment in the quality of their lives—no matter what the amount—you're being a philanthropist. Try that on. You're a philanthropist. Repeat it to yourself: "I'm a philanthropist. Me—I'm a philanthropist." How does it feel? Do you believe it?

Now, when you give your money intentionally, strategically, and consciously, you're bringing even more love to the equation. Where you put your money matters. You can be deliberate. Your giving doesn't have to be indiscriminate—determined arbitrarily by the passions of others, or by the pressing issues of the news cycle. You can be guided by your own passions. It's not just the wealthy who get to be strategic. You get to be, too.

REALITY CHECK

And *how* you give your money matters. You don't have to be bound by traditional practice and old ideas meant for another age. Your giving can be innovative— radical even—and that will make it more powerful.

So, not only are you a philanthropist, you can actually *reinvent* what it means to be a philanthropist. That's not something even wealthy philanthropists think much about. I know. I have worked with many of them. Imagine being a step ahead of the Gates Foundation. In the pages ahead, I will show you how.

Don't let your giving be stuck in ideas meant for another age.

The Difference Between Acute and Chronic Issues
Empathy Today vs. Strategy for Tomorrow

We tend to lump charity into one big bucket, not thinking much about the different natures of charitable need. Sure, we know the difference between the breast cancer, hunger, and literacy causes, but what about the differences within, say, the hunger cause category—the difference between a short-term famine and long-term world hunger? Or the difference between a particular child's kidney transplant fund and finding a cure for kidney disease for every kid?

These examples demonstrate the difference between acute and chronic issues. You should distinguish be-tween the two as you think about your giving.

Yes, you'll always want to give to the acute issues as they come up—to the victims of devastating natural disasters like earthquakes and hurricanes. And you'll always give episodically to the friend who's participating in a bike ride for cancer or a walk for AIDS. But you also want to begin to think about the chronic problem (or problems) in the world or in your home town that you'd really like to address in your lifetime—about systemic, entrenched problems that require long-term heroes, heroines, and commitments. Maybe that's being a part of the effort to find a cure for pancreatic cancer or investing yourself in ending chronic homelessness in your community (rather than simply providing soup to the homeless who are in acute need today, for example).

ACUTE VS. CHRONIC

Just as there are different types of issues, there are different ways of thinking about them, and different questions to ask when considering giving. On an acute issue, you might want the majority of the money going to the cause right now. But you'd want a good definition of what constitutes "the cause." On a chronic issue, you might want a lot going into things like fundraising—that's the building of civic engagement I just wrote about above—in order to help the organization grow substantially so it can address the root problem in the long term. If you and the other pool of current givers are all there is, you can see how the organization could never conceivably get big enough to solve a big problem.

Fundraising investment allows them to find more givers.

If their current pool of givers doesn't grow, a charity can't solve gigantic problems.

Is There a Difference Between Giving to a Nonprofit and Giving to a Charity?

Yes. As I just wrote, the "nonprofit sector" pie is made up primarily of hospitals, religious organizations, colleges and universities, the arts (museums), and health and human services organizations. The health and human services organizations are the ones we typically think of as "charities." These are the food pantries, free medical clinics, homeless shelters, overseas aid providers, youth after-school programs, domestic-violence prevention and literacy programs, environmental advocates, social justice fighters, centers for the disabled, and the cure AIDS, breast cancer, and heart disease organizations. Animal rights, small community arts, and environmental organizations too.

MYTH BUSTING

Here's a surprising fact: the organizations that we typically think of as "charities" (i.e., human service organizations) only receive about 13.5% of the money donated annually to the U.S. nonprofit sector as a whole. The rest goes to the arts, colleges, hospitals, museums, and religious institutions.

To put that into even greater perspective, U.S. gross domestic product was $23 trillion in 2021. The $65 billion donated to human services charities during the same year represents about .3% of gross domestic product, or less than a third of a penny of every economic dollar, to address the needs of the most disenfranchised and underprivileged among us.

Human service organizations receive about 13.5% of the funds donated to the U.S. nonprofits each year.

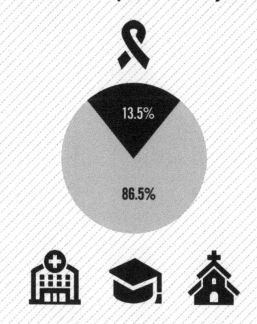

The rest goes to hospitals, higher education, museums, arts, and religious institutions.

Are All Cancer
Charities Alike?
Services vs. Solutions

N o. But that doesn't mean they're not all valuable.
They're just not the same. This is true of many
charity categories.

Some breast cancer charities provide services—like
free mammograms or supportive counseling. They
aren't doing scientific research to find a cure. Others
are *only* doing scientific research to find a cure, and
don't provide services. Some do both. Some push
for more government funding of research. None of
these are less important than the others, but they're
different. We don't often think about that. When we

hear "breast cancer charity" we think, "they're trying to find a cure." When a reporter writes that they're not, we can jump to misguided conclusions about the organization's honesty.

Some kids' charities, like Make-A-Wish, are trying to put joy into the lives of terminally ill kids or kids with life-altering diseases. That's different from a charity trying to eradicate those diseases.

Some AIDS organizations provide free HIV testing, case management, and social services. Others are trying to cure AIDS.

There are literacy organizations teaching kids how to read. There are others trying to address the causes of illiteracy at their root. A reporter might write that, "They're not even buying any books for the kids!" But they may have determined that book distribution isn't the smart path to progress.

Some homeless organizations provide temporary, emergency shelter. Others are looking at long-term solutions to end homelessness. Incidentally, the shelters might have the best field knowledge about how to end homelessness, so they may be contributing to the longer-term conversation as well.

Understand the differences between research, advocacy, and services.

 =

Research?   **Health Services?**   **Advocacy?**

Some diabetes organizations provide support networks for people with diabetes and assistance in understanding and using the latest technology. Others are trying to cure diabetes.

Get the idea?

Why Do You Give?
Do You Really Understand Your Motives?

We give money to charity because we want to make a difference in the world. Or do we? Is part of the reason we give that we want to feel good? That we feel guilty? Guilty for what we have? Guilty because we haven't given much before? Is there a conflict between these motivations?

It's easy to see how there could be. If you wanted to buy a bike at a local dealer simply because you felt guilty for not supporting the local dealer, you might be less strategic than if your motivation is to buy the best-performing, safest bike for your budget. You might buy the bike somewhat impulsively if you just need to check it off your list. You might end up with a more frivolous purchase than if you bought it because you wanted the best performance.

It works the same way with charity. Contributing $25 to a child hunger charity might make you feel good when they tell you it will feed a child for a week, but if what you're really after is ending hunger, it might not make the kind of difference you want.

Similarly, if you learn that a charity spent 30% of their money on fundraising, your unexamined prejudice might take away the good feeling you had when you gave. But what if you learned that the investment was helping them grow large enough to solve the problem and help many more people?

Anchor yourself in your reason for giving. There are difficult, entrenched problems in the world that need solving. They need champions willing to trade good feeling now for long-term, not-sexy investment, failure, trial, and error. The need to feel good now may betray your deepest intentions. Forfeiting short-term good feeling may actually satisfy your long-term strategy and make you a more valuable citizen.

The need to feel good now
may betray your
deepest intentions.

8

What's Your Cause for Life?

What issue devastates you? Breaks your heart? Makes your blood boil? On what cause would you most like to have a huge, heroic impact? Did you lose a family member or a friend prematurely to a disease that you want to see cured? Is there some issue of social injustice or inequity that has always touched you? Are children your cause?

Are you interested in a popular cause or do you want to champion some underdog cause—one that struggles to find support? Maybe it hasn't affected you at all. Years ago our company produced heroic civic journeys for important causes. We did a grueling bike ride across

Alaska in which 1,500 average people—definitely not pro cyclists—took part. It was to address the AIDS crisis in Africa and to fund vaccine research. One of our promotions said, "We're riding for total strangers. We hope, if the tables were turned, that they would ride for us." Do you want to get involved in a cause that needs you like that?

Are you interested in a local, national, or global issue? Is there a physical or mental health issue that you live with personally? What's an issue you could speak about with the most passion and knowledge?

Ponder these questions. Live inside of them for a few weeks—a few months, even. Try one out for a while. If it doesn't feel quite right, make another choice. The answer will come. And you'll be a better citizen and giver for having had the patience to wait for it.

After considering all of this and landing on a cause, consider making that your *cause for life.* Tally your lifelong contributions to it, in money and time. Set annual goals for your giving. Set goals for the impact you'd like to see in your lifetime. It's your legacy. If you focus your giving on one cause, your financial impact will be greater than if you spread your giving across a dozen issues.

In addition, the more you dedicate yourself to one issue, the more you'll learn about it. Set aside time to

**What issue most moves you?
Health? Arts? Children?
Local? Global?**

meet with leaders of the organization you're supporting to learn about their progress. Read about the cause and the issue regularly. Your understanding about that issue and your ability to speak articulately and persuasively about it to others will grow over time, making you an even better giver and a better asker when it comes to getting others to give. All of this will become a gathering and growing source of personal pride for you in your citizenship and your life.

Being a great citizen makes you feel great about yourself. It brings a feeling of meaning to your life and a feeling of purpose and place in civil society. It confirms that you matter to the person that matters most—you.

And this practice will introduce you to other people of great depth and feeling, who also feel impassioned about the cause.

Life is short. Our time and money are limited and precious.
Keep asking yourself,
"What's my cause for life?"

Part Two

Good Information Gathering

Find a Great Organization

Once you know what you want your philanthropic impact and legacy to be, commit yourself to determining what organization can help you realize it. First, research it—like you research which home or car you will buy, or which presidential candidate you will vote for. Yes, you have a right—and really a responsibility to your own hard-earned money—to explore what different organizations do and how good they are. This may be new for you, but you'll learn valuable, interesting, and important things. It will be fulfilling.

Don't rush it. You could make this a year-long project, if you like. Giving yourself time will make it seem less intimidating and overwhelming.

How, exactly, do you research an organization? What are the right questions to ask? To whom should you put them? The answers are up ahead.

The Three Essential Questions

When you're considering giving to an organization, you'll want to ask them the following three questions, thoroughly, consistently, and systematically:

1. What are your goals?
2. What progress are you making toward them?
3. How do you improve?

That's it.

These questions allow you to investigate something you may not have considered but is the most sophisticated thing to explore: an organization's intentions. That's a much more substantial domain than their financials, their overhead, their salaries, or, believe it or not, even their effectiveness. Intention tells you about an organization's character. That, more than anything else, is what you want to query. And it will put you on the bleeding edge of smart, modern philanthropy.

And it's doable.

Ask the organization:

1. What are your goals?
2. What progress are you making toward them?
3. How do you improve?

First Question: Goals

You ask about goals because you want to know, first, if the organization has any, and then, if the goals inspire you and demonstrate that the charity is accountable to something big. An organization that says, "Our goal is to improve literacy for every kid in this city by 50% in the next five years" (and means it) has a lot more on the line than one that says, "We are battling illiteracy in children."

Here are a few examples of organizations that have great goals to which they're holding themselves accountable:

FIND OTHERS LIKE THESE

- Share Our Strength has the goal of ending child hunger in America by 2030.

- Sightsavers has the goal of ending trachoma, one of the oldest diseases known to humanity and that causes blindness, in 80% of the countries in which it is endemic in five years and the remaining 20% in the five years following that.

- One Acre Fund has set a goal of serving 1.25 million farmers in five years.

You can see how these organizations are accountable to something. When the time comes, people can ask them, "Did you do it?" And the answer will be very clear. Their willingness to put their reputations on the line and be held to account says a lot about their intentions. Even if some don't reach their goals, that doesn't indict them. They will learn a lot about *why* they did not—far more than if they had never set a deadline for themselves. Armed with their new knowledge, they can set a new deadline. They can keep their intentions alive.

There are too many organizations sailing along on poetic messages of "hope" or "someday." But no one can be held accountable to "hope" or "someday."

John F. Kennedy used to tell a famous story about a kid who had a hat that he loved and a wall that he couldn't climb. So one day he threw his hat over the wall, because he knew that doing that would force him to figure out how to scale the wall. Something big was at stake.

What does the organization you're looking at have at stake?

Also, when you ask about goals, ask in a way that allows you to understand if they're serious about them, or if the goals are just part of a well-meaning, but ultimately public relations exercise. Does everyone in the organization know about the goals, or just the CEO? How did they arrive at them? Why these goals and not some others? Is the organization literate about the domain of their goals?

12

Second Question: Progress

You ask about the progress the organization is making to see if they're aware of and care about that. It's OK if they're not making progress, as long as they are intending to make progress and are honest about it when they aren't getting where they want to be. Most social problems are unspeakably tough to solve, and they require a lot of failure before there's success. Success and failure can be hard to measure. If an organization is mentoring teenage gang members, it could take years to find out whether the mentoring actually had a longstanding impact on a person's life. And it could take years to find out if it may have had a detrimental effect in some way. We expect cancer researchers to fail all day long. That's because we understand that failures are the only path to success for cancer research. Thomas Edison said, "I haven't failed. I've found a thousand ways that don't work." That's the perspective we want to have on the charities trying to solve tough social and community problems.

You wouldn't want to judge an organization simply for its innocent failures. If you met Jonas Salk, the doctor who developed the vaccine for polio, a year before he found the polio vaccine, you might be tempted to say he wasn't very effective. But that wouldn't be true. They key would be to understand his intentions—to find out if he really seemed to care about finding a cure for polio, as opposed to just caring about getting your money or getting an "A+" from an overhead watchdog agency. The key would be to see if he was learning from his failures, and to know whether he knew and cared about the difference between his failures and his successes.

" I haven't failed.
I've found a thousand ways
that don't work."

Thomas Edison

THE EVERYDAY PHILANTHROPIST

Third Question: How They Improve

Last, you want to ask how an organization knows whether or not they are making progress. An AIDS researcher does experiments and documents the results to find out if she's making progress. Charities working on homelessness or the prevention of abuse against women or anything else have to be held to the same standard. You're looking to see if they are rigorous about studying the effects of their own work, and if they change their approach if they learn something isn't working. More important, you want to know that they know when something isn't working, so you're sure they have an indicator that tells them to stop doing it and to try something else. And you want to know that they know when something *is* working, so they can do more of it.

Implicit in this question is another question, which is, What's your idea? Does the organization have a powerful—maybe breakthrough, big, disruptive—idea about how to solve the problem? An idea that they have tried and that has shown serious promise? Something no one has tried before? For example, the Bail Project looked at pre-trial incarceration in a new way. They saw that innocent individuals were pleading guilty to crimes they didn't commit simply because they didn't have the money to pay bail. Incarceration was jeopardizing their employment, housing, and ability to care for their children. This gave prosecutors unfair leverage over them. Prosecutors could easily get people to plead guilty to crimes they didn't commit with the promise of getting the whole nightmare over with. The Bail Project's idea was to provide small loans that people could use to pay bail, eliminating prosecutorial leverage. Before, 90% of people pled guilty. Now, 50% of the cases in which someone got a bail loan get dismissed. Only 2% result in a jail sentence. And there is a 96% payback rate on the loans.

That's a disruptive innovation. That demonstrates a real intention to have a huge impact on the issue. But a note of caution: you also want to watch for any unintended consequences associated with the disruption. Are any of the people being released a real danger to society who may commit violent crimes while released?

What is the organization's idea? Do they have a powerful new approach to a stubborn social problem? Something they've tried and that has shown serious promise? Something no one has tried before?

Here's another example. One Love Foundation is attacking domestic violence by teaching kids in high school about the early warning signs of relationship abuse. They use contagious video content—created by Apple's ad agency—that kids share with their friends. It's been viewed over 100 million times. Nearly a million kids have participated in one of their live workshops.

Again, you can see how the existence of a disruptive new idea demonstrates intention in and of itself.

Is the organization you're looking at just doing the same thing they've always done, without any evidence that it actually works? Are they trying to sell you on how low their overhead is in order to distract you from the fact that they haven't had a new idea in ages and they don't really measure their progress?

How can you, as a donor, find out about this? It's fairly simple. Ask whether the charity gathers data on their program effectiveness. Both the Bail Project and One Love have data that allows them to evaluate their effectiveness and see where there's room for improvement.

Is the organization sleepwalking or excited about creating real change?

Ask how many people they have gathering data and how many people they have analyzing it. Ask how they gather the data about whether their programs are working or not, and what they do with that data. Ask for some examples of the data. If they are a social service agency and they say they survey their clients, ask to see the survey. If they say they don't, what does that tell you?

DON'T SCROLL RIGHT DOWN TO FINANCIAL PAGES.

To whom do you pose these three questions? Start with the organization's annual report, which you can usually find on their website. Don't scroll right down to the financial pages to look at their overhead ratio. That's what we've all been taught to do. But we'll discuss below why that's the wrong approach. Search for the answers to the three questions. Then perform a healthy review of their website. Does it impress you? Is there data that's easy to understand, like, "50% of the cases are dismissed once people get a bail loan?"

Next, call the Development Director (that's the person in charge of raising funds). Ask for a meeting and a tour. Tell them you're looking for a charity to support for the long haul. Don't tell yourself you're wasting someone's important time. It's their job to meet with people like you and teach them about the organization's work. They'll welcome it. If they don't, you know you've got the wrong organization. When you meet, ask them about their goals and progress. Use your intuition. Does the organization seem authentically

Call the organization's Development Director. Ask for a meeting or tour. It's their job. You wouldn't be shy about asking a car dealer to take you through the features of a new car you might purchase. Don't be shy about asking a charity to extend you the same courtesy before giving—before making an impact purchase.

committed to solving the problem? Do their stories inspire you? Do their numbers? Someone once said, "no numbers without stories, no stories without numbers." Take that advice.

Do they have the information readily available? Are you convinced that they are well-intended and sophisticated enough for you to make an investment in them?

Ask the three questions. Then listen up. And continue to ask these questions as your relationship with the organization grows.

Don't Rely on Others for Simple Answers

Human beings are addicted to simplicity. Be wary of simplicity. Don't go to a charity rating agency and make a 20-second decision based on how many stars they give an organization, or whether they give them an "A" or an "F." It's not nearly as simple as that, and any group or agency that tells you it is, is selling you a bill of goods. Sometimes they're simplifying things because they can sell simplicity, and because simplicity is cheap to produce.

BEWARE OF SIMPLICITY ADDICTION

Unfortunately, none of the popular charity rating agencies has a staff that actually researches charitable program impact directly—in other words, the actual good being done (or not being done). The rating agencies are actually very small. The largest among them only has about 20 staff. Some have only one or two. It's not their fault that they're tiny, but they are tiny. And no tiny organization can put together meaningful, comprehensive, well-researched, up-to-date information about the goals and progress of tens of thousands of charitable organizations.

There are 1.5 million nonprofit organizations in America. Twenty people is one person for every 75,000 of them. If you do the math, it means each rating agency staffer would have to come up with a meaningful, in-depth assessment of a charity's work, programs, data, and effectiveness in a matter of seconds, for every working hour of every working day. Even if you reduce things down to the tens of thousands of operating charities, you can see that two or three people simply cannot cut it. Because measuring impact takes more effort than they have the capacity to undertake, many of the watchdogs rely on inexpensive, easy-to-acquire financial information, which, as we'll see, won't serve you.

You would never go to a car rating agency and buy your car because it got four stars from a rating agency without ever driving the thing yourself, right? You would never vote for a presidential candidate who had a four-star rating without listening to him or her speak, or watching him or her debate, would you?

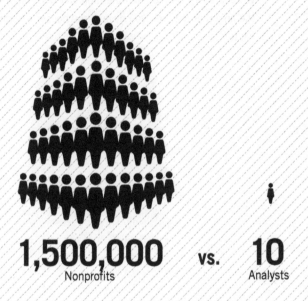

1,500,000 vs. 10
Nonprofits   Analysts

The largest of the charity rating agencies only has about twenty staff, and fewer than ten analysts. They gather financial and governance data, but they don't have anywhere near the resources they would need to measure the most important thing—a charity's impact.

You might say, "If a grading system based on overhead ratios is all they have, I guess I'll just have to go with that." But that would be like taking your child's temperature with a broken thermometer because it's the only thermometer you have in the house. You might kill the kid.

Part Three

Good Information Filtering

Don't Be Duped by Dumbed-Down Data

Don't Be Duped by Dumbed-Down Data

Questions
NOT to Ask

Here are two questions that won't give you any information about what good is being done by a charity:

What is your overhead?
How much do you pay your CEO?

This surprises you, right? All your life, these are the questions you've been told that you should ask. And you've been told this by the news media and by your attorney general. And these are the answers charities post on their websites before you even ask the questions. How is it possible that they're the wrong questions?

We might also ask, how is it possible that we walked
around the airports for decades dragging the luggage
before it dawned on us that we could put wheels on the
suitcases? And how is it possible that once we put two
wheels on the suitcases it took us another 30 years to
realize we could put four?

Human beings tend not to think about things outside
the narrow focus of their lives.

Let's look at what's wrong with these questions.

**Questions you've been taught
were helpful but are not:**

1. What's your overhead?

**2. What do you pay
   your CEO?**

Stop Asking About Overhead

You've been taught that low overhead means a lot of good is being done. This is not true. Don't take my word for it. Some of the charity rating and evaluation groups even banded together to make a major announcement on the subject:

MYTH BUSTING

"To the Donors of America: We write to correct a misconception about what matters when deciding which charity to support. The percent of charity expenses that go to administrative and fundraising costs—commonly referred to as 'overhead'—is a poor measure of a charity's performance...many charities should spend more on overhead...The people and

*communities served by charities don't need low
overhead, they need high performance."*

Charity Navigator
Better Business Bureau Wise Giving Alliance
Guidestar

The head of the Ford Foundation, one of the largest
foundations in America, said this:

*"Nonprofit watchdog groups...have equated lower
overhead with organizational effectiveness when, in
fact, the opposite may be true. At Ford, we have been
willing participants in this charade. Our policy of 10
percent overhead on project grants in no way allows for
covering the actual costs to administer a project. And to
be honest, we've known it."*

Darren Walker, President, Ford Foundation

In late 2019, five of America's big foundations—Ford,
MacArthur, Packard, Open Society, and Hewlett—
banded together to say they were going to start funding
much more overhead in an effort to destigmatize
overhead spending and help people understand how
critical it is to impact.

Why would these people and organizations finally be
acknowledging this? Let's see...

Overhead is a poor measure of a charity's performance... many charities should spend more on overhead."

Charity Navigator
Better Business Bureau Wise Giving Alliance
Guidestar

Overhead Ratios Tell You Nothing About Impact

When a charity tells you that 95% of every dollar goes to the cause, you think that means they don't waste money, right? Wrong. How do you know they're not wasting the 95% they tell you they spend on the cause? That's where all the money goes! That's where they have the biggest chance to waste money! Imagine two soup kitchens, A&B: A tells you 90% goes to the cause, B tells you 70%. You think you should give to A, right? Not so. What if A is serving expired soup from cans, has a rude staff, a kitchen infested with rodents, and only serves 50 people on Fridays? But B has nutritious soup, a friendly staff, and serves thousands every day. The low overhead at A would have have betrayed you.

MYTH BUSTING

OVERHEAD DOESN'T MEASURE WASTE

**MYTH
BUSTING**

**OVERHEAD
DOESN'T
MEASURE
GOOD**

A close friend of mine just quit her job working with a children's agency because she didn't feel the work she was being given was stimulating for the children. One hundred percent of her salary was allocated as going to the cause. But it wasn't actually helping the cause. You can see how asking how much money goes to the cause doesn't help you to understand the impact of your donation on that cause. You need different questions, like the three mentioned earlier.

You want to find out what good is being done, not what the overhead is. Look for the good and for the good intentions.

More often than not, to do a lot of good, a charity has to invest more in overhead. The ones that tell you they have no overhead are probably not investing in the training of their staff, the quality of their programs, their innovation, their growth (which is key to reaching everyone affected), or the other things it takes to do a lot of good and to do it really well.

You would never ask, "How much was the overhead on this mobile phone?" before you buy it. That would be the last thing you'd be interested in. You would want to find out how well it functions. That's exactly what you want to do before you give money to a charity.

A survey conducted for the Better Business Bureau Wise Giving Alliance asked people what they most

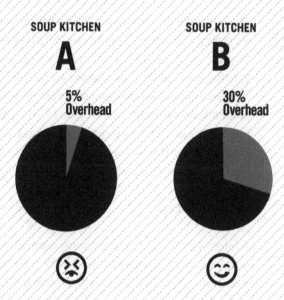

SOUP KITCHEN
A

5%
Overhead

SOUP KITCHEN
B

30%
Overhead

What if Soup Kitchen A has lower overhead than B, but A serves watery soup to a few dozen people, while B serves hearty soup to thousands? The overhead question would have hidden that information from you.

86%

wanted to know what percentage of their donation was spent on overhead.

BUT ONLY...

6%

wanted to know if their donation *made a difference.*

want to know before donating to a charity. About 86% of people said they want to know what percentage of their donation is spent on overhead. Only 6% said they wanted to know if their donation made a difference.

Why is that? Do donors not care whether their donations are making a difference? They do care. But by telling people to ask about overhead ratios all the time, and by telling them that the good charities are the ones with low overhead, we have managed to convince the public that the two things are the same. So, if they ask about overhead, they think they don't have to ask about impact, because they've been taught that low overhead = great charity = big impact.

But it isn't the case.

An email I got from a former employee exemplified a dangerous public mythology: "You see, for every dollar a donor gives they have the expectation that it's used efficiently. After all they have choices, they can give that same dollar to another charity. Donors want their donations to go as far as possible..."

There are two fatal errors here. The first is, again, that high administrative efficiency (aka "low overhead") equals high impact. It doesn't. The second is that the overhead ratio is measuring efficiency. If it isn't measuring impact, it isn't measuring efficiency, because the only efficiency that matters is how efficiently you achieve impact! Take the frugal, low overhead breast cancer charity that consistently fails to make progress toward a cure for breast cancer. The last word a woman dying of breast cancer would use to describe it would be "efficient."

As for making donations "go as far as possible," think about the example of the two soup kitchens. The overhead ratio is completely void of any information about which soup kitchen is better at serving soup. And yet, we praise it as a yardstick of morality and trustworthiness. It's the exact opposite.

We should stop saying charities with low overhead ratios are efficient. Efficient at what? Fundraising? What we have been taught to call "inefficient" fundraising may actually raise a lot of money and accelerate problem solving, making its "inefficiency" efficient in the big picture.

That was a big sentence.

Let's try it this way. Say Jonas Salk spent $50 million to raise $100 million to find a polio vaccine—people would say he had a shameful 50% overhead. His fundraising was very inefficient, they would say. But the $100 million he raised wasn't his end result. It's the wrong denominator. His end result was a vaccine for polio. Let's use the real end result as a way of measuring his fundraising efficiency. Divide the $50 million

THE CHARITY THAT *DIDN'T* FIND THE CURE FOR POLIO GETS LABELED "MORE EFFICIENT"!

fundraising expense into the God-only-knows-how-many billions of dollars a polio vaccine is worth, and his overhead ratio at eradicating polio is very close to 0%. A hypothetical goody-two-shoes competing charity with a 10% fundraising cost that comes up empty on a vaccine has 100% overhead against the goal of a vaccine, because it never found one. But it's labeled the more "efficient" charity! As one of millions of people spared a polio diagnosis because of Salk, I'd have to disagree.

In 1995, Physicians for Human Rights had revenues of approximately $1.3 million. They spent approximately $750,000, or 58% of revenues, on programs. Today that organization would fail all of the watchdog standards for efficiency. It would be ineligible for a watchdog seal of approval. But the Nobel Peace Prize committee felt differently. Physicians for Human Rights won the Nobel Prize in 1997 for its work as a founding member of the International Campaign to Ban Landmines.

We take huge pride in giving to charities with low overhead without knowing a thing about whether they're any good at what they do. You don't have to fall for that anymore.

The email from my former colleague was right in one respect. As a donor, you do have a choice. And it's in your best interest to stop using the hallucinogenic "overhead" measure to determine how to make it.

" My organization can give you 5% overhead and never significantly impact child hunger in America, or we can give you 35% overhead and eradicate child hunger in forty out of fifty states and counting. Which would you prefer?"

Bill Shore, CEO, No Kid Hungry

Overhead Ratios Weaken Charitable Services and Programs

When a charity becomes obsessed with keeping overhead costs down, they often forgo investment in the essential people, equipment, and training required to provide good services to their clients and/or to make solid progress toward their goals.

The Nonprofit Overhead Cost Study conducted by Indiana University explored what can happen when incentives are twisted to reward how little a charity spends rather than how much it achieves. They pointed to a specific case of "a hotline that could not afford to upgrade its phone system—an expense that was considered part of overhead. Without this upgrade, a suicidal caller could get a busy signal, even though some hotline extensions were not busy. It is hard to imagine a better example of sacrificing the mission on the altar of low overhead."

In other cases, the study observed that: "Nonprofits in the arts, community development, and human services describe how their development efforts were hindered by inappropriate donor database software. One site described the unproductive downtime and frequent maintenance associated with 'free' but mismatched, outdated computers. In agencies where key positions such as development director either did not exist or were filled with inexperienced staff, the CEO had to fill that role, thereby neglecting parts of the leadership role. Sites without experienced finance staff had only rudimentary financial reporting and had limited ability to involve program managers in financial management, perform more sophisticated analysis or identify financial issues for board and senior management. Backup for key roles was nonexistent, leaving basic functions like payroll, benefits, and network support dependent on a single person in even the largest nonprofits with which we spoke."

In their seminal article, "The Nonprofit Starvation Cycle" in the *Stanford Social Innovation Review*, authors Ann Goggins Gregory and Don Howard gave the example of a youth development program poised for growth, but with woefully inadequate data systems

" [In one case,] a hotline could not afford to upgrade its phone system—an expense that was considered part of overhead. Without this upgrade, a suicidal caller could get a busy signal, even though some hotline extensions were not busy. It is hard to imagine a better example of sacrificing the mission on the altar of low overhead."

Indiana University Nonprofit Overhead Cost Study

to accommodate more of the needy. They found that, "An analysis showed that program staff spent 25 percent of their time collecting data manually. One staff member spent 50 percent of her time typing results into an antiquated Microsoft Access database."

One organization they interviewed revealed that, "We [had] known for a long time that a COO was vital to our growth but [hadn't] been able to fund one." The authors noted that, "When his organization's board finally created the COO position, the rest of the staff resisted. They had lived so long in a starved organization that the idea of hiring a COO was shocking to them."

They concluded that, "A vicious cycle is leaving nonprofits so hungry for decent infrastructure that they can barely function as organizations—let alone serve their beneficiaries."

Just in these examples, you can see that it's not high overhead spending that's a waste of money. It's low overhead spending. For lack of a proper computer that costs 2% of a person's salary, 50% of their productivity is squandered. As a donor, the last thing you want is to be another source of pressure on charities to under-invest in themselves in this way. You want to be a voice for organizational power and capability, both for the sake of the charity's clients and the long- and short-term impact of the money that you're giving.

Don't be another source of pressure on charities to under-invest in themselves. Be a voice for organizational power and capability.

Overhead Measures Discriminate Against Underdog Causes

Breast cancer is a popular cause. Heroin addiction is not. A breast cancer charity may be able to run a $10,000 social media ad campaign that attracts $50,000 in donations. That's a 20% cost of fundraising. The heroin recovery charity may run a similar campaign for $10,000 and only take in $20,000 in donations, because their cause comes with stigma and isn't as popular with the public. Their cost of fundraising is 50%. They both did the same thing, spent the same money, but if you only looked at their 50% fundraising cost, you might conclude that the heroin recovery organization is misusing funds. The media might well encourage you to think that way with a story that says precisely that.

You would never want to harm an underdog cause that finds it difficult and expensive to raise funds simply because there are not many people affected by the issue. Yet that is exactly what reliance on simplistic overhead ratios encourages you to do. It encourages us to render harsh, penalizing, often moral judgment against underdog causes that are struggling to find donors.

In 1988, the Supreme Court took up the matter of a North Carolina law which stated that any professional fundraiser's fee exceeding 20% of the total funds raised was unreasonable. The law sounds more than reasonable, doesn't it? Then why did the Supreme Court rule against it, 7-2?

With wisdom ahead of its time, the Court wrote that the law, "unconstitutionally infringes upon freedom of speech. The solicitation of charitable contributions is protected speech, and using percentages to decide the legality of the fundraiser's fee is not narrowly tailored to the State's interest in preventing fraud...the Act is impermissibly insensitive to the realities faced by small or unpopular charities, which must often pay more than 35% of the gross receipts collected to the fundraiser due to the difficulty of attracting donors."

Two decades ago the Supreme Court had a better understanding of the realities of nonprofit business practice than many of even the wealthiest donors do today.

Since "efficiency" ratios are based in large part on fundraising costs, they inherently discriminate against less popular causes, causes with less affluent constituencies, and new charities. At every level, it's more expensive for a less popular cause to raise money than it is for a popular cause. The less popular cause has to spend more on education and solicitation over a longer period of time for each dollar it raises, while the popular cause may see money coming in over the transom, at zero cost, because, for example, a donor just lost a loved one to breast cancer. How many people have lost a loved one to polluted oceans or illiteracy?

Similarly, an inner-city addiction recovery clinic without access to the millionaires who give to the art museum will have to rely on direct mail and special events, historically the most expensive ways to raise a dollar. A Giving USA study found that every $1.00 spent to solicit major gifts yielded $24 in donations, the highest performance on their list of methods. Direct mail—those solicitations that come in your mailbox—produced only $10 in donations for every $1.00 spent. Special events produced $3.20. The less access a charity has to major donors, the less it can take advantage of inexpensive fundraising methods, so many small, community-based organizations have to resort to bake sales, casino nights, and phone banks—which all come with higher overhead and fundraising costs. Last, a new nonprofit that lacks the

REALITY CHECK

CHARITIES IN POOR AREAS MUST RESORT TO HIGH OVERHEAD METHODS TO RAISE MONEY

established donor database of an older organization will have to spend more money building one.

The "low overhead" game is stacked against charities working on the issues for which it is hardest to find support. The nonprofits representing the popular issues are doubly blessed. They get relatively easy money, and then they're praised by the establishment as "efficient," while those addressing the issues for which it is most difficult to raise money are slandered as "inefficient," making what was a hard case for support to begin with an impossible one in the end.

This is not what you want. It's not what you ever intended.

The supreme law of charity violates the supreme law of the land. And the Supreme Court vote on the matter wasn't even close.

The "low overhead" game is stacked against charities working on the issues for which it is hardest to find support. It makes our generosity unjust.

Overhead Measures Weaken Civil Society and Diminish Civic Engagement

We've all been taught that when a charity spends a lot of money on fundraising, they are wasteful. We don't like it. We want our money to go to the cause.

It's unfortunate that we use this narrow word, "fundraising," to describe an activity that is much broader, more beautiful, and rich in scope than the simple transfer of money. When an organization spends on fundraising, it's spending money to get people off of their couches, away from their TVs and devices, and active in some cause. It's educating them. It's waking them up. It's trying to encourage them to get involved in the great social struggles and challenges of our time.

Imagine if we had an America where everyone was aware of, active, and contributing to the cause of their lives. That's exactly what charities are trying to achieve when they spend money on fundraising.

When we contribute to a political campaign, we expect the campaign to spend virtually all of its money trying to create awareness about the candidate, and get people to participate in their society—get them out of their houses to vote. Why wouldn't we encourage the same kind of grassroots organizing when it comes to cancer, violence against women, poverty, and illiteracy?

When my company produced the AIDSRides and the Breast Cancer 3-Day walks in the 1990s and early 2000s, the money we spent on overhead and fundraising was labeled as some kind of a necessary evil. Some people wondered whether the "necessary" part was even true. They wished that the $585 million we raised over nine years could have been raised without spending a penny—without even having to conduct the events.

182,000

NEW CIVIC HEROS AND HEROINES

But guess what that money, that some would say didn't go to the cause, went to. It got 182,000 people in America to do something extraordinary for others, the likes of which they had never done, or considered doing, before in their lives. It got tens of thousands of people to ride their bicycles across Alaska, Montana,

Imagine if we had a world in which everyone was aware of, active in, and contributing to the cause of their lives. That would take a big investment.

Texas, Minnesota, and Wisconsin. It paid for the salaries of hundreds of full-time employees who recruited, nurtured, and supported those heroes and heroines. It gave thousands of people who were HIV positive the experience of a lifetime, surrounded by tens of thousands of people showering them with love and support. It got tens of thousands of people to walk for 3 days and 60 miles in cities all over America to show their support for thousands of breast cancer survivors—who found new sustenance and inspiration by being surrounded by all of this love and support.

And it got three million Americans to write checks. These events raised more money, more quickly, for AIDS and breast cancer than any events in history. In other words, its getting-people-off-their-couches power was off the charts.

When we discourage charities from spending money on what we call "fundraising," we are discouraging this kind of magical, critical, phenomenal strengthening of American civil society.

But does our mindset actually discourage charities from spending on fundraising? It does. I am involved in an initiative that curates very exciting, innovative, multi-million-dollar charitable projects from very innovative organizations. The initiative encourages charities to dream really big. These projects are then presented to ultra-high-net-worth individuals for funding consideration.

Three million people donated to the AIDSRides and Breast Cancer 3-Days as a result of significant investments in stimulating civic engagement. That's enough people to fill about 46 football stadiums.

In our last go-around, seven of the ten finalists, and all of the finalists that have websites (some are brand-new ideas that don't yet exist), either specifically highlight and/or otherwise communicate their low spending on overhead and fundraising to donors, either on their home pages or on their donation pages. Two carry a prominent watchdog's seal of approval and promote the fact that they have that evaluator's highest rating—much of which is a reward for low administrative and fundraising expenditures. The other four all try to reassure donors by showing or telling them that their fundraising costs are less than 6% of their budgets. For one, the costs are only 1%.

So, two organizations are comforting donors with a seal of approval that amplifies inaccurate ideas about how charities should be measured, and five have fallen into the trap of under-spending on fundraising to attract donors.

 None of these incredibly innovative organizations can build the civic engagement and support they need to take their ideas into the big leagues with this kind of under-investment. Is it any wonder that they can't change the world?

Building a stronger civil society is a critical role of the nonprofit sector. Who else will ever do it? As a donor, you want to encourage the organization that you pick to invest money smartly in engaging other people on a broad scale. If you really want to be an effective philanthropist, consider funding this function yourself—perhaps exclusively—for the organization that you really love. This will multiply the impact of your money, because it will bring in new money. Multiplication is the single smartest practice in which a philanthropist can be engaged. Yet very few do it because of the traditional bias against it.

Multiplication is the single smartest practice in which a philanthropist can be engaged. Yet very few do it because of the traditional bias against "fundraising" spending.

Overhead Measures Hide Unfair Differences in Accounting

The percentage of your donation that goes to the cause depends entirely on how a charity defines the cause in their accounting. And the percentage that went to overhead depends entirely on how they define overhead. When you give to the soup kitch-en, you may think that soup, and only soup, is what should be accounted for as "going to the cause." But the charity may decide that the money they spend on advertising about how much soup they serve is "going to the cause." If you don't know that, then you and the charity will have very different ideas about how much money went to the cause.

For example, if a big disease research charity stages a 10K walk and props up its reputation by telling participants, "Only 30% of donations went to expenses and 70% went to the cause!," the average person will think that 70% went to medical research. In reality, if the charity off-loaded half of their event expenses to "the cause" (e.g., if 60% of donations, not 30%, really went to expenses, but the charity labeled half of those expenses as part of "the cause"), then only 40% of donations actually went to medical research, not the 70% that the public thinks. If the charity doesn't tell you that very clearly, that's a betrayal.

I favor a broad definition of the cause. I think 100% of what charities are doing, if in good faith, is cause-related. But I have a problem with not telling the public loud and clear what that definition is.

You can see the problem that arises if one charity is doing very aggressive accounting and another is being very conservative: The conservative one looks like they have higher overhead.

Does this happen in the real world? The Nonprofit Overhead Cost Project studied the tax forms of 126,956 charities. The following findings are remarkable:

- Nearly half of the charities studied reported zero fundraising expenses. Of the larger charities with annual revenues between $1 million and $5 million,

Same Spending, Two Completely Different Pictures of What % Went to the Cause vs. Overhead

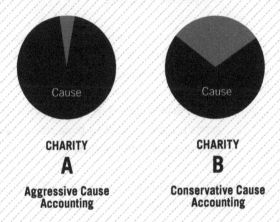

CHARITY A

Aggressive Cause Accounting

CHARITY B

Conservative Cause Accounting

If Charity A is doing aggressive "cause" accounting and Charity B is being conservative, the more conservative Charity B will appear to send less money to the cause, but it isn't true. And it isn't fair.

one-quarter reported zero fundraising expenses. How do you raise $5 million without spending a penny doing it?

- About 27% classified some or all of their accounting fees as program expenses, despite the fact that the tax form instructions give accounting fees as an example of what is meant by "management and general" expenses.

- Only 25% of nonprofits receiving foundation grants properly account for those proposal-writing expenses as fundraising costs.

- Just 17% of nonprofits receiving government grants properly account for those proposal-writing expenses as fundraising costs.

Real efficiency and the appearance of efficiency are two different things.

Why are these practices epidemic? Because we told charities we wanted low overhead. The media terrorizes them with draconian reporting on high overhead—reporting that can destroy an organization. So these organizations actually consider it a matter of survival to report low overhead. Now, they bear equal burden for not speaking up for themselves, but they are largely blinded by their fear.

We tell charities we want low overhead. The media terrorizes charities with draconian reporting on higher-overhead peers— reporting that can destroy an organization. So charities actually consider it a matter of survival to report low overhead.

A warning here: Don't use this data to tell yourself that you cannot trust charities. Use it to tell yourself that you cannot trust overhead ratios to tell you anything meaningful, and certainly not anything you can use for meaningful comparison, about the merits of a charity.

**Stop using overhead pie charts to evaluate charities.
They are a distortion.**

Overhead Measures Discourage Growth

Because charities know that the general public demands low overhead, they don't spend as much as they could or should on fundraising to raise more donations. That means they can't grow at anywhere near the rate we need them to, and therefore they can't solve gigantic social problems that require them to be much bigger. If there are 7,000 homeless people in your city and your homelessness charity is only big enough to serve 500, you see the problem.

Look at the pie charts on page 115. The bake sale on the left only has 5% overhead. The professional fund-raising event on the right has a whopping 40% overhead. "That's shameful," some people might say. And look at how much more money is going to the cause from the bake sale than the professional fundraiser!

But is it true?

It's important to notice something about the pie charts you are always shown: They always show the pies at the same size. So, you're missing the most important piece of information, which is, how big are the actual pies? What if the bake sale is tiny? What if the bake sale only sent $71.00 to the cause, because it made no investment in its growth, and the professional fundraising effort sent $70 million to the cause because it made a huge investment in its growth? On the lower right you see how the comparison should really be presented. Now which pie looks like it's sending more money to the cause? Which looks like it can feed the most people?

And think about this: When you discourage your favorite charity from spending money on fundraising to find other donors, you're actually telling them that you don't want them to find other donors. Do you really want them to rely exclusively on you and the existing pool of other donors—to have to keep coming back to you—and only you—asking you for more and more each year in order to grow? That's the exact opposite of what you want.

What You Are Usually Shown

Bake Sale
Only 5% Overhead!

Professional Event
40% Overhead!

What You Should Be Shown
(And this is not even nearly to scale)

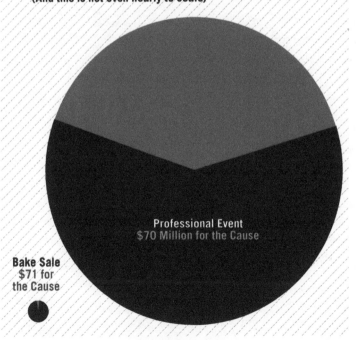

Professional Event
$70 Million for the Cause

Bake Sale
$71 for
the Cause

Demanding Low Salaries Undermines Your Strategy to Help the Most People

You want your hometown baseball team to hire the best possible pitcher and coach, no matter what the cost, so they can win, right? You're willing to pay a higher ticket price if that brings home a World Series trophy, yes? And you want them to hire a great catcher, shortstop, and so on.

Don't you want the same thing for the charity you're making your cause for life? Yes, you do!

You want them to find the best possible person, with the best leadership qualities, and the most awe-some track record at producing results, so they can win! Those people cost money. And it's not fair that corporate America gets so many of them just because we let corporate America steal them away by paying much higher salaries, offering bonuses, and providing stock. When you buy a new computer, you don't care what the computer company's CEO makes, right? You just want to be sure that CEO is leading a team that builds the best computer for your money. It's the same with charity.

But, you say, "If the CEO gets a bunch of money, that's money taken away from the cause." Not so. Not if the CEO raises a lot more money for the cause than a lesser person would.

Here's a simple way to look at it. Would you rather have a CEO who gets paid $100,000 but can only raise $1 million for the cause every year, or a CEO who gets paid $500,000 dollars but is so good that they raise $10 million a year for the cause? The "cheap" CEO raises $900,000 for the cause after their salary. The expensive one raises $9.5 million after their salary. Now who looks more expensive? If we're going to solve these gigantic humanitarian problems, we need the best people we can find. And we need to motivate and incentivize them the way we do baseball players.

Which Would You Prefer?

A Low-Paid CEO Who
Can't Get the Job Done

A CEO Who's Paid Well,
Based on Big Results,
and Can Lead the Team to
Win Against Tough Social
Problems

Which Would You Prefer?

Part Four

Good Media Consumption

Monitor Truth in Media

Be Responsible and Rigorous When Learning About Charities in the Media

The public agrees on one thing—they don't trust the media. Only 15% of Republicans and 27% of Democrats trust the national media. Only 2% of Republicans and 5% of Democrats trust social media. Only 23% of Republicans and 29% of Democrats trust the local media.

Yet when it comes to any single given story, everyone believes! Why is that? That's a subject for another book.

There's another thing on which Republicans and Democrats agree—charities waste a lot of money. It's not true, but they do agree on it. A 2018 report by Grey

Matter Research found that, "Nearly six out of ten donors feel charities typically spend too much on overhead (often by a wide margin), while just 15% feel the typical charity expense ratio is below what they consider to be a reasonable limit." They also found that, "Almost half of all donors believe their favorite charity's expense ratio is higher than it actually is, including one out of four donors who believe their favorite organization spends at least twice as much on overhead as it really spends."

PEOPLE THINK CHARITIES WASTE MONEY. BUT NO STUDIES HAVE FOUND THAT.

An NYU study found that 70% of donors believe charities waste either a "great deal" or a "fair amount of money." But there are no studies that show that charities actually *do* waste money.

So why does the public feel the way it does? Because the media keeps dripping the word "overhead" on the public's forehead, like Chinese water torture. Because the public keeps being fed, and believing, sensational stories about charities and charity overhead that scream "mismanagement" and drive clicks.

So, one of the fundamental things you can do to be a great donor is to find out the other side of the story when a charity is maligned in the media. Add a positive comment if it's warranted. Educate others. And most important, don't believe—automatically—what you read from media (that you already perhaps don't trust).

Case Study: CNN and Boys & Girls Clubs of America

In 2012, CNN's Wolf Blitzer (who, at the time, was earning $4 million a year) reported that in 2008, Boys & Girls Clubs' CEO Roxanne Spillett received a total compensation package of $988,591.

WOLF BLITZER $4 MILLION

Shocking, right? I mean, that's money that should be going to boys and girls, not into some fat cat CEO's pocket, wouldn't you agree?

CEO, BOYS & GIRLS CLUBS $988,591

Wolf Blitzer himself commented that "this is a pretty shocking story," and made sure that the story would cause great consternation by telling viewers, "This is going to cause a lot of consternation out there."

The Washington Post, *Huffington Post*, and Associated Press all picked up on and redistributed the story. This is how it works: One media outlet reports it, and others, without doing additional research or fact-checking to see if the first outlet got it right, redistribute the story to all of their viewers and readers, massively amplifying and reinforcing it until it becomes truth.

As a result of the stories, Senator Chuck Grassley of Iowa made political red meat of the organization, accusing the Boys & Girls Clubs, prior to any investigation, of "siphoning off" taxpayer money to high CEO salaries while some of the Boys & Girls Clubs, he said, are having to close because of the economy. The media also claimed that Senator Grassley was investigating because the Boys & Girls Clubs received $41 million in government grants in 2008.

This all sounds pretty bad. And if that were all you heard, that's what you'd conclude.

But how would you feel about that salary if you knew the following:

- More than a third of the salary figure was deferred compensation for back payments Spillett was owed for a retirement plan. This wasn't reported.

RETIREMENT PLAN

- During her eight-year tenure as CEO, Spillett had tripled network-wide revenues from $500 million annually to $1.5 billion annually. This wasn't reported. Imagine if the organization found a CEO for $150,000, but the person was incapable of increasing donations. You would "save" several hundred thousand a year in salary, making everyone feel good (and those hundreds of thousands could now go to the boys and girls), but you would have lost $1 billion—every single year!—in unrealized revenue. A few hundred thousand saved and a billion lost for children, annually.

TRIPLED REVENUE

- During her eight-year tenure, Spillett doubled the number of kids served by the organization, precisely because she led a massive increase in revenues. This was not reported.

DOUBLED KIDS SERVED

- On the matter of Senator Grassley investigating because the Boys & Girls Clubs received $41 million in government grants in 2008—well, at the same time, Lockheed Martin received 95% of its $42.7 billion 2008 revenues from the Department of Defense to build weapons. Its CEO's 2007 compensation was $30.1 million. Why is he not being investigated?

DOUBLE STANDARD

So, look for an organization that isn't timid about finding a CEO who can lead it to its true potential. And don't dismiss an organization just because they pay their CEO well. Find out what value the CEO is producing. Find out why the organization believes that person is worth it. Now, if they can't tell you, or if your own exploration reveals that they really aren't worth it, that's a different matter. But don't judge them without getting some facts.

The money paid to a valuable CEO is not money taken away from the cause. It's an investment in the cause. How many clubs would have had to close if the Boys & Girls Clubs had been without an effective CEO, or if it paid a person half as much and only got half as much productivity? Is the money paid to Disney's CEO seen as denying kids more affordable access to Disneyland? Is Wolf Blitzer's salary ever framed as "siphoning" money from consumers, forcing some to go without cable television?

Senator Grassley and Wolf Blitzer wanted to frame this as a moral issue. But the real moral issue is that in one 24-hour news cycle, they manufactured a massive public relations and fundraising nightmare for the Boys & Girls Clubs, without the slightest effort to evaluate the CEO's compensation in the context of the value she was providing. Any first-year business school student who tried to make a case against an executive salary without a shred of cost-benefit analysis would be laughed out of class. The effects of such reckless finger-pointing reach far

In one 24-hour news cycle, sensational, incomplete reporting can create a massive public relations and fundraising nightmare for a great charity.

beyond the Boys & Girls Clubs. These attacks bring down the image of the sector as a whole, reinforce the widely held public view that good organizations waste money—and make it harder to raise money overall.

The worst thing that could have happened here would have been for the Boys & Girls Clubs to succumb to the pressure and cut its CEO's pay, or worse, force a resignation in the interest of public relations without regard to the value proposition, as so often happens in these cases.

What did happen? Roxanne Spillett was forced to resign.

Don't contribute to the illiteracy that can cause something like that to happen.

Your literacy is the antidote.

Case Study:
The New York Times and
Wounded Warrior Project

I n January 2016, *The New York Times* and CBS News
released high-profile, sensational investigative reports
on Wounded Warrior Project—the large veteran's
charity. They called the organization's big fundraising
expenditures into question. CBS News stated, "What
caught our attention is how Wounded Warrior Project
spends donations compared to other long-respected
charities." They compared Wounded Warrior unfa-
vorably to others, showing how low a percentage of
donations others spent on fundraising, and how high
a percentage Wounded Warrior spends. They accused
them of "lavish" spending in non-program areas—alco-
hol purchased with donor money at big employee par-

ties, first-class air travel by executives, and the like. *The New York Times* reported that they found "many current and former employees questioning whether [Wounded Warrior Project] has drifted from its mission."

By combining and sensationalizing two spending areas, a picture of systemic over-spending and donor betrayal was painted, damning the fundraising spending in particular.

Donors were outraged.

But how would you feel about Wounded Warrior Project if you knew these things:

MASSIVE GROWTH

- Fifteen years ago Wounded Warrior Project didn't exist. By 2014 they were raising, $400 million a year with over $242 million a year available for veterans' services. They represented 40% of private philanthropy for veterans in America. This was not reported. This is exactly the kind of Apple-like, Amazon-like growth we need in our charitable sector, yet they were criticized for investing in making it happen.

MORE MONEY FOR VETERANS

- Other veterans' charities spend a lot smaller percentage of donor dollars on fundraising than Wounded Warrior Project. For 2014/2015, another organization—Semper Fi—spent just 2.4% of donor dollars on fundraising. Another—Disabled

American Veterans Charitable Service Trusts
(DAVCST) —spent just 1.2%. Wounded Warrior
Project, by comparison, spent a whopping 14.5%.
Those are the only types of numbers that the
media highlighted. But guess who had more money
to spend on veterans? DAVCST had $6.5 million.
Semper Fi had $23 million. Wounded Warrior
Project had an unbelievable $242 million, for that
year alone. Which approach is going to reach more
veterans? Which is more likely to solve the big
problem of veterans not having mental health and
job training services?

- Remember the pie charts we looked at that showed
  the bake sale against the professional fundraising
  enterprise? Here's what it looks like if we compare
  Semper Fi and Wounded Warrior Project:

**HONEST PIE
CHARTS**

Semper Fi
2.4% Fundraising Cost
$23 Million for Veterans

Wounded Warrior
14.5% Fundraising Cost
$242 Million for Veterans

HUGE IMPACT ON VETERANS

• Prominent language on the Wounded Warrior Project website indicated that during the period in question, Wounded Warrior Project assisted over 100,000 warriors and family members through 20 programs and services, served over 45,000 warriors and family members through health and wellness programs, secured over $160 million in benefits for warriors and their families, and that its advocacy resulted in legislation that paid over $2 billion to warriors and their families. Neither report mentions these statistics. Additionally, Wounded Warrior Project's audited financial statements provide granular narrative detail on each of 16 veterans programs. Neither report discussed these programs in any detail.

CENSORED

• A prominent video on Wounded Warrior Project's "Mission" website page describes how they measure impact. No information about this was included in the reports.

90%-95% CUSTOMER SATISFACTION

• Remember how we talked about gathering data to measure impact? Wounded Warrior Project asked clients to complete customer satisfaction surveys. Client satisfaction with alumni events and services was 92.9%. There were 50,603 in-bound contacts to its Resource Center with a 90% satisfaction rate. Their Project Odyssey mental health support program served 2,668 warriors and caregivers with a 98.1% satisfaction rate. And 1,845 veterans and

Neither *The New York Times* nor CBS News reported the 90% + customer satisfaction rates from tens of thousands of veterans, despite that information being prominent on Wounded Warrior's website.

caregivers were served through Soldier Ride, with a 94.8% satisfaction rate. It was all on Wounded Warrior Project website. Yet none of it was reported.

- *The New York Times* stated that "Former workers recounted buying business-class seats and regularly jetting around the country for minor meetings." Wounded Warrior Project's Board conducted a forensic audit of expenses. It found that 99% of all air travel at the organization was coach class. Less than 1% was *upgraded* international travel to provide urgent services to veterans overseas. There was no first-class travel by the CEO. Which raises another point. Many charities have restrictions on first-class travel. Some allow business class travel for executives so they can be productive and prepared for meetings they might be traveling to. Meanwhile, corporate executives travel in private jets with private catering.

Nevertheless, as a result of the stories, Wounded Warrior Project's board announced on March 10, 2016, that its CEO, Steve Nardizzi, was "no longer with WWP"—despite being cleared of any mismanagement by a financial audit. We make sacrificial lambs of our most effective CEOs because they violate antiquated ways of thinking. You can speak out about organizational behavior like this. It diminishes the impact of your giving.

**Wounded Warrior Project
was a model of audacious
growth and impact
measurement. This is the
kind of bravery you want
to stand for, not against.**

Case Study: ProPublica on the American Red Cross

On June 3, 2015, ProPublica published a story on the Red Cross' Haitian relief efforts with the headline, "How the Red Cross Raised Half a Billion Dollars for Haiti and Built Six Homes." The subheading reads, "Even as the group has publicly celebrated its work, insider accounts detail a string of failures..."

The Washington Post borrowed the headline virtually verbatim for its June 4, 2015, story: "The Red Cross had $500 million in Haitian relief money, but it built just 6 houses." *The Post* interprets the headline literally, stating that, "That's just over $83.3 million a house, according to my iPhone calculations." It says that, "the big takeaway from ProPublica's latest Red Cross investigation which explores how the international charity grossly mismanaged its response…"

MISLEADING REPORTING GONE VIRAL

The Chicago Tribune picked up on the narrative. Al Jazeera reported that, "New report alleges US aid group raised almost $500m but only managed to build six homes in country devastated by quake." From *Time* on June 3, 2015: "Red Cross Spent Half a Billion Dollars to Build Six Homes in Haiti." And on Salon.com on June 7, 2015: "The Red Cross' Haiti disgrace: Half a billion dollars spent, six homes built."

Here's some of what the public had to say in response:

"Man, if you can't trust the Red Cross…Yet another example for my growing mistrust of ever giving to any charity."

"I believe what they do the best these days is PR, the FBI should stay home and investigate these people, this is a lot of money we're talking about here."

"You just need to form charity networks, using the transfer of assets that are harder to steal from. Instead of cash, sending packages of canned goods, sending packages with tents, and supplies to build basic structures for housing…"

"How sad—and sadly unsurprising—to find out that the Red Cross is just another player in the Big Rip-Off of

American consumers (once known as "citizens") by the shrewd exploitation of nonprofit incompetence and foreign misery. If you could track how the money was actually spent, you would find that nearly all of it has gone into improving the neighborhoods of suburban Washington, DC."

"Shameful. That's why I don't donate because of greed among the charity and the workforce. Someone needs to go to jail for this. So glad Red Cross is destroying its trust among the public."

And you would probably agree, if all you read were the papers, right?

American Red Cross

But how would you feel about the Red Cross if you knew these things:

- With the half billion dollars they raised, the Red Cross did much more than build six homes.

  BEYOND HOMES

- They originally intended to use most of the money to build homes, but then decided that they could help many more people with a different strategy of repairing existing homes.

  REPAIRS

- They repaired and retrofitted homes and provided rental subsidies and relocation for 54,125 people (ProPublica makes one mention of the repair of 4,000 homes and another mention of the improvement of 5,000 temporary shelters).

  RELOCATIONS

- They provided transitional shelter for 30,850 people.

  SHELTER

- They upgraded shelters for 25,130 people.

- They performed neighborhood renovations in the form of roads, bridges, sanitation, electricity, and more for 21,794 people.

  RENOVATION

- They supplied more than 70% of the funds needed for Haiti's first cholera vaccine, which reached 90,000 people and supported cholera treatment centers. (ProPublica simply mentions that the Red Cross has a cholera vaccination campaign.)

  VACCINE

- They provided help in repairing, constructing, or operating eight hospitals and clinics, including a

  HOSPITALS

$5.5 million contribution for Mirebalais University Hospital, run by Partners In Health, and paying the salaries and operating expenses for 27 months at Bernard Mevs Hospital Project Medishare, to ensure services were not interrupted. (ProPublica simply says that the Red Cross constructed one hospital.)

JOBS

- They spent or committed $48 million to job training and creation, cash grants, small business support, and other livelihood programs in Haiti.

HYGIENE

- They provided water, sanitation, latrine construction, waste collection, and other hygiene-promotion services to 556,000 Haitians, complementing the Red Cross housing work. (ProPublica simply mentions a Red Cross hand-washing education campaign, without citing any figures.)

TARPS

- They provided temporary shelter in the form of tarps to 860,000 people.

FUNDING

- The stories brush right past the fact that the Red Cross did indeed raise half a billion dollars, as if that wasn't an accomplishment in and of itself. But anyone who understands fundraising understands what a massive achievement it is to raise $488 million quickly, and at low cost. To raise that much money with normal fundraising costs of 15%–25% would have cost close to $100 million alone. The Red Cross, because it's the Red Cross, did not have to spend that. In the absence of its powerful fundraising capability, none of what the Red Cross achieved would have been possible. This fact is never acknowledged by ProPublica.

- While $488 million is an enormous amount of money to raise through fundraising, it's not an enormous amount of money up against the scale of 1.5 million people left homeless by a devastating earthquake. The unrelenting negative tone of the ProPublica story gives the implication that the Red Cross should have transformed Haiti. Ten million people live in Haiti. $488 million is just $50 per person. It's a statistical zero against the scale of the population. The ProPublica story quotes dissenters exclusively. It's no surprise that, in a poor country ravaged by earthquake, with woefully inadequate resources to get back on its feet, there would be a healthy supply of disenfranchised people—an abundance of people with expectations of the Red Cross and others that were too high to begin with or could not otherwise be met. The media doesn't address this.

A LOT WITH A LITTLE

- Disaster relief work is messy, and no two disasters are alike. Language barriers, government turnover, land title issues, pressure to spend money quickly, and physical distance all contribute to making it more difficult. It's not like stamping out iPhones, where this one will be manufactured in precisely the

IT'S MESSY

same way as the previous one. It's not as simple as writing a news story. So it should not be news that there were problems and disagreements. It's the nature of that kind of work. While ProPublica mentions that other groups had difficulties, it does not name them. Nor does it investigate them. And the overall tone of the story is anything but sympathetic to the challenges the Red Cross faced.

In emphasizing—through its headline—that the Red Cross should have built permanent homes, the ProPublica story removes itself from the ethical dilemma in the room, which is, what's better, to build several thousand homes, or to help hundreds of thousands of people? And who is to decide who gets a new home and who gets nothing?

Part Five

Are
We Good?

It's Time to Rethink Charity

For well over a decade, it's been popular to preach to charities that they should act more like businesses, but the truth is, society won't permit it. What we mean by "act more like business" is really "focus more on lowering overhead"—the opposite of what it takes to grow a successful business.

The nonprofit sector remains tightly constrained by a set of irrational economic rules handed down to us through the ages—rules that discourage profit, self-interest, serious marketing, risk-taking, and long-term investment for growth. These rules work against the sector on every level, and they have been elevated to the status of "ethics."

The nonprofit sector is in an economic prison, and the for-profit sector roams the economy free as a bird. The very system we have established for rectifying inequity in society is treated inequitably—across every meaningful domain.

FOR-PROFIT ADVANTAGE

We let the for-profit sector pay competitive wages based on value, but have a visceral reaction to anyone making a great deal of money in charity. We let people make a fortune doing things that will harm the poor, but want to crucify anyone who wants to make money helping them. This sends the top talent coming out of the nation's best universities directly into the for-profit sector, and gives our youth mutually exclusive choices between doing well and doing good. It's not sustainable, let alone scalable.

FOR-PROFIT ADVANTAGE

We let Coca-Cola pummel us with advertising, but donors don't want important causes "wasting" money on paid advertising. So the voices of our great causes are muted. Consumer products get lopsided access to our attention, 24 hours a day. Charitable giving has remained constant at about 2% of GDP ever since we've measured it. Charity isn't gaining market share. How can it if it isn't permitted to market?

FOR-PROFIT ADVANTAGE

We let for-profit companies invest in the long term to identify new sources of revenue, but we want charitable donations spent immediately to help the needy. No won-

We allow for-profits to shout at us with billions of dollars in beautifully produced advertising so we'll buy their products, but we don't want charities to spend money telling society their stories, so they can't get us to "buy" the way for-profits can. This is why we have so much more consumption than compassion.

der charities can't scale to the size of the social problems they confront.

FOR-PROFIT ADVANTAGE

We aren't upset when Paramount Pictures makes a $200 million movie that flops, but if a charity experiments with a $1 million fundraising event that fails, we call in the attorneys general. So charities are petrified of trying bold new revenue-generating endeavors and can't develop the powerful learning curves the for-profit sector can.

FOR-PROFIT ADVANTAGE

We let for-profit companies raise massive capital in the stock market by offering investment returns, but we forbid the payment of a financial return in charity. The result? The for-profit sector monopolizes the capital markets, while charities are left to beg for donations.

This isn't what any of us wants. So why do we have a system that works this way? It dates back to the Puritans. They came to the new world for religious reasons in the 1630s. But they also came here because they wanted to make money. These meek, humble, prayerful people were also extremely aggressive capitalists. But they were Calvinists. So they were taught—literally—to hate themselves. They were taught that self-interest was a "raging sea that was a sure path to eternal damnation."

This created a real problem for these people.

The nonprofit sector is in an economic prison while the for-profit sector roams free as a bird. Is it any wonder nonprofits can't get big enough to change the world?

Here they had come all the way across the Atlantic to make all of this money, and making all of this money would get them sent permanently, immediately, and directly to hell. This created enormous psychological tension. And there wasn't a therapist anywhere to be found.

What to do?

Charity became a big part of their answer. It became this economic confessional in which they could do penance for their profit-making tendencies—for five or ten cents on the dollar—without stopping their profit-making tendencies. So, of course, how could you make money in charity if charity was your penance for making money to begin with?

And in 400 years, no one has intervened to say, "Wow, that is really dysfunctional."

It's not 1630 anymore. This system no longer serves us. It's killing people. It's time to give charity the big-league freedoms we really give to business. The fight for these freedoms must be our new cause. That fight is the best fight a great giver can engage, because without these freedoms, all of our causes are ultimately lost.

Recap

Here's a cheat sheet on what we've covered:

- The way we've been taught to think about charity and giving is insanely counterproductive.
- Charity is an important platform for creating change.
- Giving is critical to fueling the kind of change we want to see.
- The way we've been taught to think about our roles as charitable givers and active citizens is also misguided.
- You are a philanthropist. You get to be strategic and deliberate. You can change how we think about change.

- There are acute and chronic causes, services, and solutions.
- There is a difference between the nonprofit sector and "charity" as we often think of it.
- Know your motives for giving.
- Contemplate what your cause for life will be.
- Find a great organization.
- Ask these three questions:
    1. What are your goals?
    2. What progress are you making toward them?
    3. How do you improve?
- Don't over-simplify or trust those who do.
- Don't ask about salaries without asking about value.
- Don't ask about overhead. Ask the three questions instead.
- Overhead tells you nothing about impact, it discriminates against underdog causes, it weakens civil society, it discourages growth in civic engagement, it hides accounting differences, and it enables damaging over-simplification by sensational media.
- Don't believe by default all that you hear and see about charities in the media.
- It's time to rethink our whole philosophical approach to charity and giving.

Remember what we said at the beginning. Charities aren't changing the world the way we had hoped they would because that's not what we asked them to do. We asked them to keep their salaries and overhead low. So that's what they did. Your job as a true philanthropist is to support them by giving them the freedom they need to create real change, whatever that takes.

CHAPTER

30

You

Thank you for being a citizen already concerned enough about the world around you to invest the time in reading this book to learn how you can do even more to make a difference in our world. It's a testament to your commitment to possibility. As a person committed to possibility, I have to say, the world would be a very lonely place without people like you.

Afraid You'll Forget?

If you forget some of what you've just read, flip through
the book again from time to time. And remember the
following—you can cut it out and keep it in your wallet:

**I don't want my tombstone to read, "I Kept Charity
Overhead Low." I want it to read, "I Changed the World."
So I should ask about the good and the growth, not
the overhead.**

And if you want to go really deep, you can read the
much longer book I wrote on the subject for Tufts University Press, recently reissued by Brandeis University
Press, entitled *Uncharitable*. It is available from all of
the major online book sellers.

Want to See It on Film and Video?

In 2013, I gave a talk at TED on these ideas. It became very popular, with millions of views. It's 18 minutes long and will help give you a context for everything you've read here. It's called, "The Way We Think About Charity Is Dead Wrong." It's also a great tool to send to friends who may need convincing. It's convinced a lot of people!

TED

It's free and you can find it here:
https://www.ted.com/talks/dan_pallotta_the_way_we_think_about_charity_is_dead_wrong

If you work for a nonprofit organization or sit on the board of a nonprofit organization and want to take your board and staff deeper into these issues, and get them all aligned on a bold vision for making an audacious impact in your community and in the world, there's another powerful tool you may find valuable. It's called, "The Bold Training for Nonprofit Boards and Staff." I present these live and in-person as a one-day workshop. But because it's been so popular, I've also made it available online as a beautiful and inspiring course, divided conveniently into seven modules that you can watch at your own pace. To learn more or to register for the online course at any time, visit https:// theboldtraining.com.

Finally, my book, *Uncharitable*, has been made into
a powerful documentary movie with the same title.
It's extremely persuasive, emotional, and inspiring.
It features the leaders of TED, the Ford Foundation,
No Kid Hungry, Charity:Water, the YMCA of Great-
er Chicago, One Love Foundation, the Bridgespan
Group, the actor Edward Norton, and many others.
It's an incredible tool for changing the thinking of the
ecosystem around you. You can learn more at
https://uncharitablemovie.com.

UNCHARITABLE
THE MOVIE
Everything You Know About
Change . . . is About to Change.

Find out where to watch at:
https://uncharitablemovie.com

Thank You

Special thanks to Stephanie Tade and Christina and Colleen at the Stephanie Tade Agency for believing in this project and for helping to shape it. Especially grateful to Stephanie Tade for the beautiful and pithy title! Thanks to Brian Neill for his persistence in pursuing this beautiful reissue by Wiley. Thanks to Paiwei Wei for the handsome design and thinking of denim, and to Ali Meghdadi and Julie Sullivan for the copyediting and other suggestions. And to all of the participants in the Bold Trainings for Nonprofit Boards and Staff who inspire me to continue to want to change the world's mindset on this most important of all matters. Last, thanks to Jimmy and the kids for opining on ribbons and for reading and for making it a better world for me everyday.